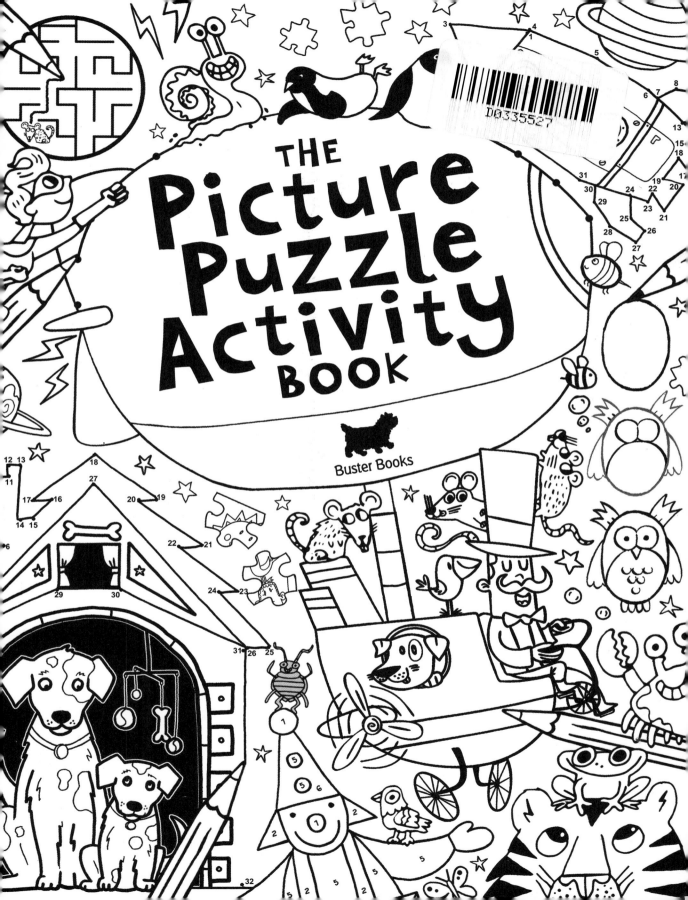

The Picture Puzzle Activity Book

Buster Books

ILLUSTRATED BY
JAMES COTTELL, CHRIS DICKASON,
ANDREW GEESON, EMILY GOLDEN,
JON MITCHELL, ALEX PATERSON,
ANDREW PINDER, AMI-LOU SHARPE
AND THE BOY FITZ HAMMOND

EDITED BY JOSEPHINE SOUTHON
DESIGNED BY JACK CLUCAS
COVER DESIGN BY ANGIE ALLISON

This edition first published in Great Britain in 2020 by Buster Books,
an imprint of Michael O'Mara Books Limited, 9 Lion Yard,
Tremadoc Road, London SW4 7NQ

 www.mombooks.com/buster   Buster Books   @BusterBooks

The material in this book previously appeared in *Buster's Brilliant Dot To Dot*, *Clever Kids'
Book of Fun*, *Dot To Dot*, *Meerkat Mischief* and *The Big Busy Book*.

ISBN: 978-1-78055-668-0

2 4 6 8 10 9 7 5 3 1

This book was printed in November 2019 by Leo Paper Products Ltd,
Heshan Astros Printing Limited, Xuantan Temple Industrial Zone,
Gulao Town, Heshan City, Guangdong Province, China.

Copy the elephant into the grid below.

Join the dots and colour the scene.

4

Spot the odd one out in each row and colour it in.

Find and colour four matching pairs of seahorses.

Which seahorse doesn't have a twin?

Find and colour
five matching pairs
of seashells.

Which shell doesn't
have a partner?

Use wild wiggles to make amazing manes.

One of these superheroes doesn't have a twin. Which one is it?

10

Shade the superhero pairs in matching colours.

Colour the tigers using the number code below.

1 = orange   2 = black   3 = green

Join the dots and colour the scene.

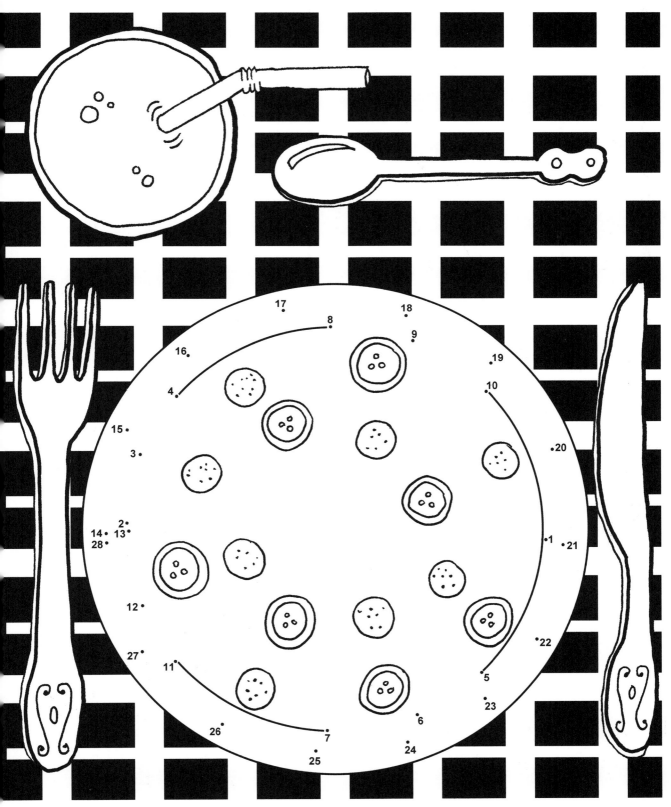

Spot the odd one out in each row and colour it in.

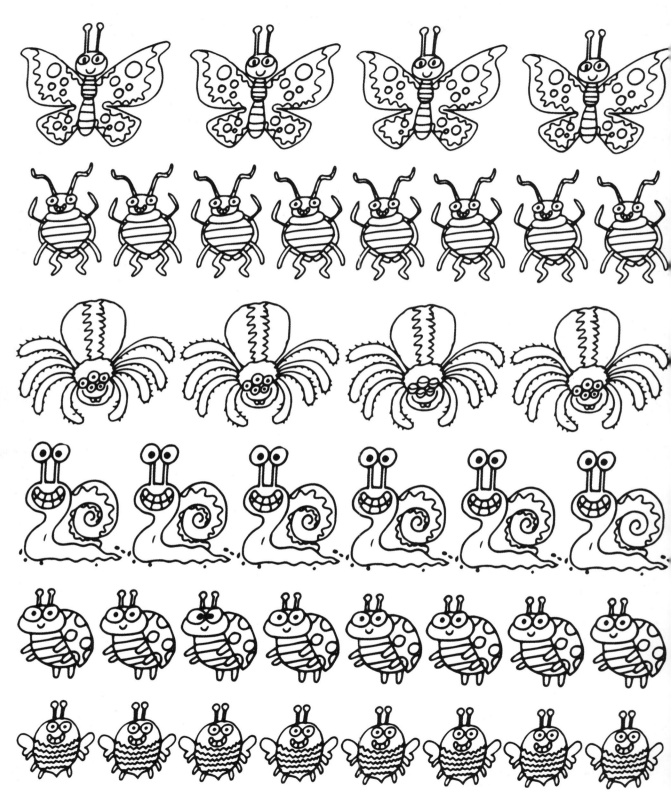

Join the dots ... ... and colour the scene.

15

Colour two sweets red.
Colour four sweets blue.
Colour three sweets yellow.
Colour one sweet green.

How many sweets have not been coloured?

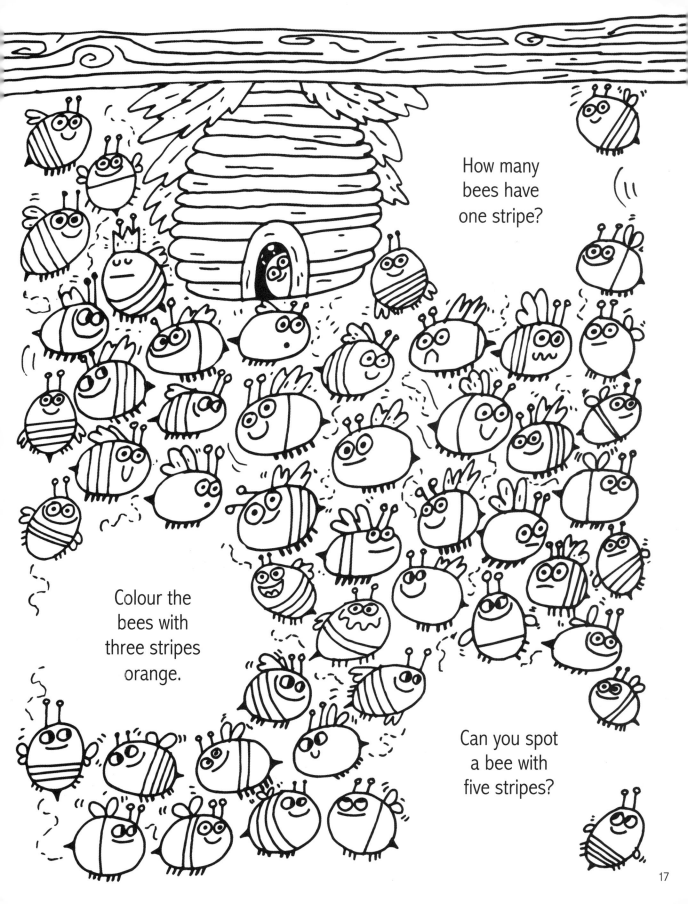

How many
bees have
one stripe?

Colour the
bees with
three stripes
orange.

Can you spot
a bee with
five stripes?

Follow the steps to draw a rocket.

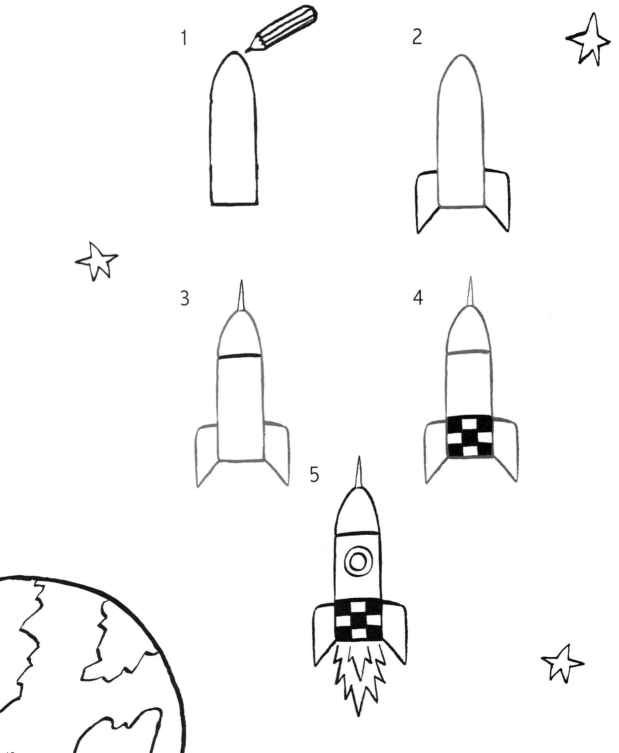

1

2

3

4

5

Now colour it in.

19

15 meerkats have sneaked into this theme park.
Can you spot them all?

Can you complete these shell sums?

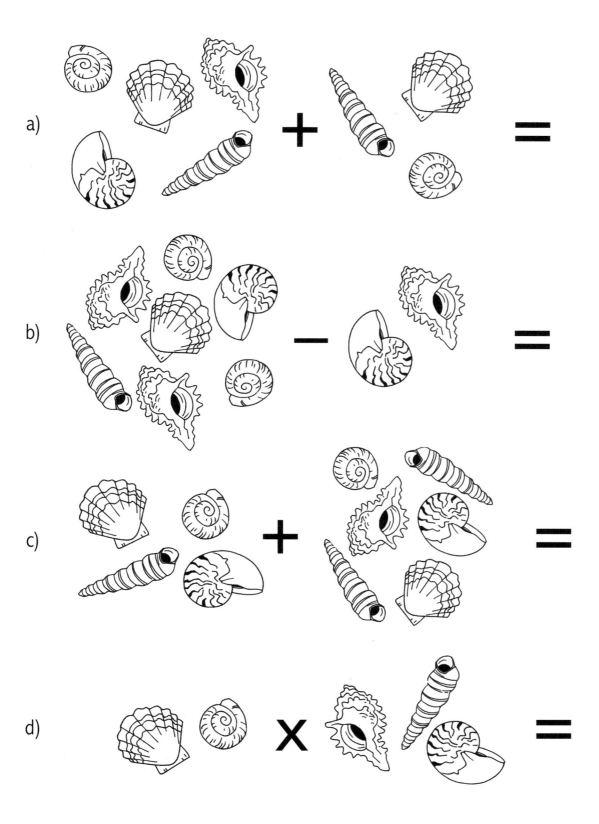

How many flowers can you find?
Colour them pink.

How many frogs have spots?
Colour them all green.

Colour two sleeping
lizards orange.
How many sleeping
lizards are left?

23

Join the dots and colour the scene.

24

Finish

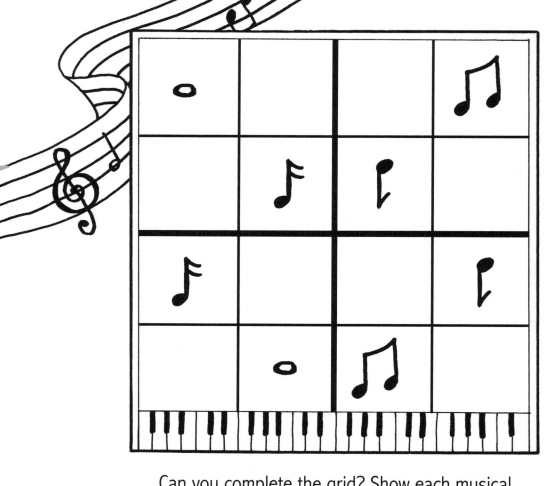

Can you complete the grid? Show each musical
note only once in every row, column and mini grid.

Add more musical notes to this picture.

Colour in the shapes containing dots to reveal the animal.

Join the dots and colour the scene.

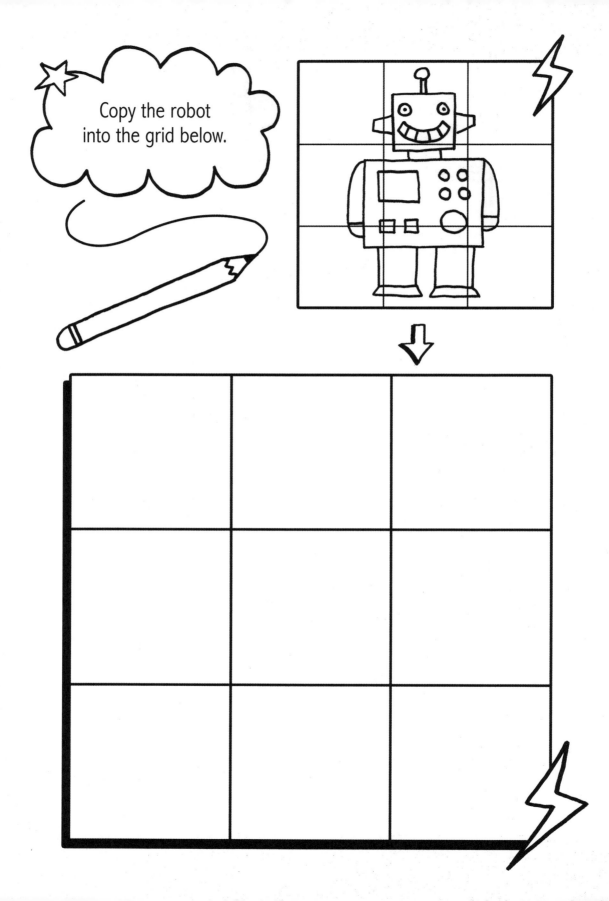

Copy the robot into the grid below.

Colour the sections using the key below.

1 = yellow   2 = brown   3 = blue
4 = red   5 = pink   6 = orange

Join the dots and colour the scene.

Which house will get which gift?

Follow the steps to draw an owl.

1

2

3

4

5

Now colour it in.

Join the dots and colour the scene.

How many fish can you find?

How many baby penguins can you count?

How many seals can you spot?

Join the dots and colour the scene.

42

There are six differences between these two market scenes. Can you spot and circle them all?

Colour the fruit and vegetables.

Follow the steps to draw a squirrel.

1

2

3

4

5

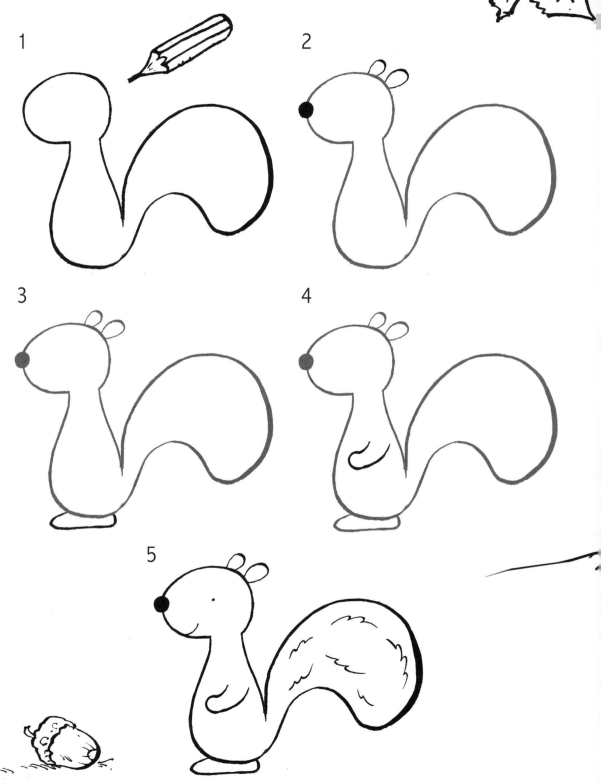

Now colour it in.

Which piece completes the jigsaw?
Can you draw it in?

a

b

c

d

e

f

Copy the dinosaur into the grid below.

Match these monsters into
gruesome twosomes.

Colour all of the
monsters with two
eyes blue.

50

a

b

c

d

e

Colour the monsters with the most eyes green.

f

There are ten differences between these two clock scenes.
Can you find and circle them all?

Join the dots and colour the scene.

Scribble some big squirts of water.

Join the dots
and colour the scene.

58

Only one chest contains pirate treasure.
Follow the clues below to find which one it is.

Colour the sections using the key below.

1 = red   2 = orange   3 = purple
4 = pink   5 = blue   6 = yellow

All the answers

Page 5

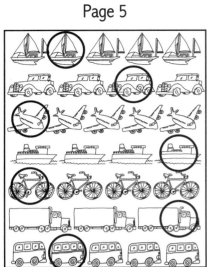

Page 14

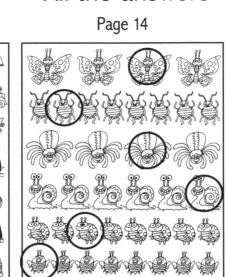

Page 16

Two sweets have not been coloured.

Page 17

There are 12 bees with one stripe.

Pages 6–7

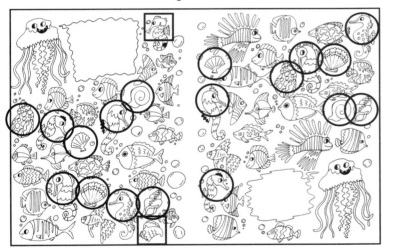

Page 20

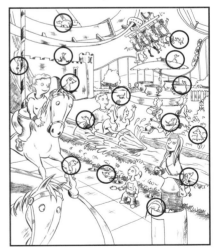

Page 21

a) 8, b) 5, c) 10, d) 6

Pages 22–23

There are 14 flowers.
10 frogs have spots.
There are 3 sleeping lizards left.

Pages 10–11

Pages 26—27

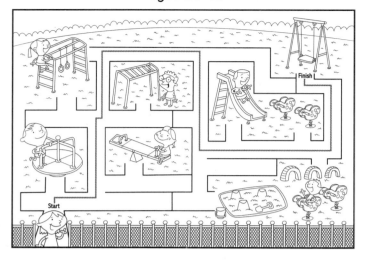

Page 28

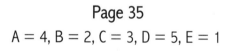

Page 35

A = 4, B = 2, C = 3, D = 5, E = 1

Page 39

Pages 40—41

There are 9 baby penguins,
5 fish and 3 seals.

Pages 44—45

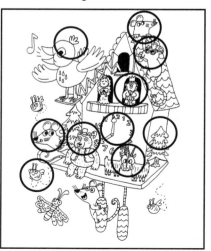

Page 48

Piece d completes the jigsaw.

Pages 50—51

a) 3, b) 6, c) 4, d) 5, e) 1, f) 2
f and 2 have the most eyes.

Pages 52—53

Pages 60—61